ALSO BY JAMES D. BEST

<u>The Steve Dancy Tales</u>
The Shopkeeper
Leadville
Murder at Thumb Butte
The Return
Jenny's Revenge
Crossing the Animas
No Peace

<u>Other Novels</u>
Tempest at Dawn
The Shut Mouth Society
Deluge
The Templar Reprisals

<u>Nonfiction</u>
Principled Action
The Digital Organization

Collaborative Works

Wanted, A Western Story Collection

Wanted II, A Western Story Collection

Miracles and Massacres

Being George Washington

PRAISE

"The James Best books ... are about the best new western series to come along since Larry McMurtry." *True West Magazine*

"You'll find yourself lost in the book—the fast pace keeps it interesting." Maritza Barone, *Woman's Day*

"James D. Best has written at least six books. I read them and enjoyed them immensely." Gary Clothier, *Star Democrat*

"This is a fast-paced tale with an interesting hero ... you'll certainly find enough twists and turns to provide an entertaining and exciting story." Western Writers of America

"A lively, old-fashioned style Western—clever, entertaining, and full of period references to give it authenticity. Best paces his stories so well readers will find it difficult to put down." Diane Scearce, *Nashville Examiner*

"A great book; I do hope that *The Shopkeeper* gets the readership it richly deserves." Simon Barrett, *Blogger News Network*

"Once again, Best has penned a fine read." *Roundup Magazine*

"I loved it! The story is told in such a classic, smooth tone—it's really fast paced throughout." Jonathon Lyons, Lyons Literary

"James D. Best is arguably one of the best writers of westerns." Alan Caruba, *Bookviews*

"They are just excellent reading." *Holgerson's Book and Bookstore*

"This is a compelling narrative and as good as the best of classic westerns. James D. Best is a name to remember." *Saline River Chronicle*

"The writing is clear and straightforward with plenty of action attached. For an entertaining read, *The Shopkeeper* draws high marks." T. Akery, *'Bout Books*

"Great stories, interesting and diverse characters and plenty of action! I have enjoyed every one of them. I can't wait for the next one and hope it comes soon!" Larry Winget, NYT/WSJ bestselling author

"The Steve Dancy series is as good as they come." *Roundup Magazine*

"Best's writing style is a romp, and he nails the dialogue. Two thumbs up!" Leadville Laurel, Leadville Literary League

"The best novel EVER on the U.S. Constitution." Larry Schweikart, professor of history and author

A Patriot's History of the United States and a dozen other history books

"If you want to know the truth about the character of those gentlemen and you want to learn about the evolution of one of the greatest documents ever created by man---the Constitution of the United States---relax in your bed, favorite chair or recliner, and enjoy."

Allen Ball, *Beaufort Observer*

"Thanks to James Best's masterpiece, *Tempest at Dawn*, I felt like the 56th delegate at the Constitutional Convention. Vivid narrative and expressive dialogue." Michael E. Newton, author *The Path to Tyranny, Angry Mobs and the Founding Fathers, Alexander Hamilton*.

"The novel captures the real drama that ensued behind closed doors as they hammered out what is now the oldest living constitution and the foundation of the nation. Read it for its historical value. Read it for its dramatic value. But read it!" Alan Caruba, *Bookviews*

"*The Shut Mouth Society* is a fast-moving, well-written novel." David M. Kinchen, *Huntington News*

"The author has done an excellent job of building the story." *Book Advice*

"*The Shut Mouth Society* is the kind of book I like best. The novel has everything from intrigue and murder to romance." Faith Friese Nelson, *A Writer's Journal*

"Best makes *Deluge* a compelling—indeed frightening—story. This is a highly recommended natural disaster thriller, written with acute attention to reality and little, if any, needless melodramatics." Jack Rochchester, *The Fictional Cafe*

WRITE GREAT FICTION

Tips from the Best Writers in History

James D. Best

Queen Beach Publishers

Sherlock Holmes, James Bond, Hercule Poirot, Elizabeth Bennet, Tom Sawyer, Captain Ahab, Rhett Butler, Hannibal Lecter, Steve Dancy, and Harry Potter

Friends, one and all

CONTENTS

FOREWORD

In their own words, the masters will explain how to write a page-turning novel. They'll discuss writing, not selling. Many books purport to tell aspiring authors how to sell their product. This is not one of those books. I wanted to get that out early in case you wanted to request a refund.

In a way, this book is about selling books. Despite what the marketing gurus tell you, word-of-mouth is still the greatest selling tool for fiction … and the only way to get good word-of-mouth is to write an engaging story. The marketeers give the impression that sprinkling social media glitter over your work will generate untold riches. Not true. For one thing, social media strategies are passé three nanoseconds after a how-to book hit the shelves. The internet moves at near light speed. What worked last month is superseded by a new twist the following month. Besides, these supposed experts never reveal their very best techniques. They keep those stratagems to themselves because they know overuse erodes effectiveness.

Don't get me wrong, you will need to use social media and every other selling technique, but internet extravaganzas, personal appearances, and advertisements are meant to put enough copies in readers' hands so that word of mouth gets rolling. A successful launch is not enough. You need a product so good that early adopters tell their friends, family, and co-workers about your great book. That's how books go viral. When real people, face-to-face, tell others about your books, sales multiply on their own. You don't want fans; you want to turn your readers into your personal sales force. You can flog a poorly written book forever, but sales will always flounder after an initial burst of buying.

Don't despair. These masters will help you write the kind book that will generate great word-of-mouth.

Are You Made Out for Writing?

This is an important question you should ask yourself before committing countless hours to the craft. There's simple test I can illustrate with a story. One time at a writers' conference, someone in the audience asked how I got inspired. I was about to give a cockamamie answer but decided to be honest. I told her that if she was searching for a way to become inspired, she probably was not a writer. Writers love to write. I told her I could write for ten minutes or six hours. I could write in a noisy coffee shop or my quiet den. When I was writing, I never heard what was going on around me. Time evaporated. Writers don't need inspiration; they need more time. I know a writer who has sold over one hundred million books. He's nearly eighty but writes nearly every day. He's obviously not doing it for the money.

Writers never stop writing. If you do what you love, then you want to do it all the time. That's why when a writer dies; his or her heirs discover at least one unfinished manuscript. Writers write right up to the end. (Robert Ludlum and a few others apparently developed the knack to write from the grave.)

This is how I answered the questioner. She looked crushed.

I needed to rehearse a cockamamie answer to that question.

1 — FIRST, TELL A STORY

Storytellers command attention. That's their job. Storytellers first went to work around a fire in prehistoric times. Cave painters did their illustrations. In fact, despite contrary assertions, storytelling may be the world's oldest profession.

Aspiring writers frequently agonize over words, sentences, and paragraphs. They want to get the tiniest piece right. Because they admire a great writer's style and distinctive presentation, they believe the technical aspects of writing are foremost. They're not. Storytelling is foremost. Great writers first understand the art of storytelling, then concentrate on telling stories in a fresh and pitch-perfect manner. After all, no matter how pretty your sentences, you must keep readers interested or they'll wander off to parts unknown.

Stories can be told many ways. The oral tradition goes back to the dawn of time. Plays extend almost as far back, epic poems have been around for millennium, and we've had novels for centuries. The twentieth century brought us stories on radio, television, and at movie houses. The twenty-first century inured us to short, short stories with tweets, blogs, YouTube, GIFs, stand-up comedy, and other tiny bits of narrative.

A story doesn't need to convey some vital message, encourage social change, impart a crucial moral lesson, or reveal a fresh truth. Stories can and often do accomplish these things. Philip Pullman once wrote, "Thou shalt not is soon forgotten, but Once upon a time lasts forever." Throughout the ages, societies have used fiction to transmit culture and traditions to the next generation. But stories don't necessarily need a higher purpose; they can also just entertain. Readers laugh, cry, and get excited when immersed in a story. Most important of all, they relax by venturing into another world; a world that certainly has problems, but these are not the same problems they must deal with in their own lives.

What constitutes a story? Kurt Vonnegut is one of the best writers of the 20th century and he had a simple perspective on stories. "Somebody gets into trouble, gets out of it again. People love that story. They never get sick of it."

Why did I start this book by discussing storytelling? Because storytellers know how to command attention. This is a book about how to turn your novel into great fiction. That means you want attention. To get attention, you must learn the art of storytelling. Your novel can be literary or erotica, but when all the refinements are taken away, it's a story. It must be interesting ... and it must transport your reader into a world you invented.

There are many who think a literary novel should never stoop to the tricks employed by genre writers. William Shakespeare would disagree. Shakespeare wrote to entertain, to draw crowds into the theater to see his shows. In his day, he was not a literary figure; he was the equivalent of a prim-etime screenwriter. A paying audience was crucial because around forty people depended on his plays for their livelihood. If he wrote a flop, his troupe and their families went hungry.

Shakespeare was a great writer and a consummate storyteller. It's the combination that makes him world renown nearly 400 years after his death. Raymond Chandler, one of my favorite writers said, "All art at some time and in some manner becomes mass entertainment, and that if it does not it dies and is forgotten."

Shakespeare is remembered because he told engaging stories. From an artistic standpoint, he was an unbelievably gifted wordsmith, but word craft alone did not make him immortal. Nor will great storytelling without serviceable writing skills. Stories that last generations are interesting *and* well written.

There is no shame in aiming for a large audience. Whether you write literary fiction or genre stories, you want readers … as many as you can get. Writing formulistic tripe will not gain a big audience. You can't load up a fantasy novel with unpronounceable names, weird creatures, and odd terrain and expect six figure sales at a buck ninety-nine. It's not going to happen. Unless … unless you tell a good story.

Storytelling trumps writing. Just ask Harold Robbins, Danielle Steel, or Dan Brown. They all got rich writing pabulum. If you're young, you may wonder who Harold Robbins was. He died in 1997. He wrote 25 bestsellers and sold over 750 million books, ranking him as the fifth bestselling author of all time. Robbins was a great storyteller, but less than gifted writer. As a result, he built a solid following that withered away after he quit pumping out one book after another. Immortality eludes slipshod writing.

With that in mind, let's start with William Shakespeare.

Chapter Links

Kurt Vonnegut four-minute definition of storytelling   http://www.youtube.com/watch?v=oP3c1h8v2ZQ)

2 — WILLIAM SHAKESPEARE

Writer's Digest did a piece titled, "10 Things Shakespeare Can Teach us About Writing Thrillers." The ten tips help every genre. Notice that all these tips gleaned from Shakespeare have to do with the storytelling side of his great talent. Here's a synopsis of the article.

Conspiracy. Murder. Politics. Love. Sex. Ghosts. Pirates. Thrillers and the works of William Shakespeare may have more in common than you'd think. As author A.J. Hartley proved in his session "Cues from Shakespeare, the First Thriller Writer," there's a lot the bard can teach about storytelling.

1. Good writers borrow ... Great writers steal.

Most of Shakespeare's stories originated in other source material. "This is just kind of the nature of the beast," Hartley said—there's a limited number of original tales out there. So, great writers steal "and then own the result."

Shakespeare wrote his works in his own way, with his unique signature.

2. Remember: Shakespeare never went to Italy.

Without delving into the Shakespearean authorship question, how could the son of a glove maker evoke settings, fields, and time periods he couldn't have ever experienced? "By reading. Copiously. Diligently." Writers should never let their research trump their tales. Shakespeare gives you as much as you need to tell the story, and that's all.

3. Get right to it.

Shakespeare doesn't waste time getting things moving. Any book should do the same.

4. Story is character.

In the bard's world, the props and costumes are kept to a minimum. The plays can be performed on a bare stage. "It's all about the interaction between character and how the characters speak." Likewise, from a story perspective, a thriller shouldn't be about explosions and car chases, but character.

5. Begin scenes late and end them early.

Just like the screenwriting maxim.

6. All scenes must have external and internal conflict.

It's not enough for the door to be locked. The character must have a reason to not want to open it.

7. Pace isn't speed.

"Don't be afraid to slow down to focus between action and event." Hartley noted that people tend to talk about the need for books to go fast. What sets Shakespeare apart is that he allowed his characters to register the events that happened to them "for the emotional and spiritual consequences of things to land."

8. Bad things happen to good people.

Shakespeare gets his audience to love his characters, and then he kills those characters off. The result: You're always in fear. "It's a brilliant, simple story strategy," Hartley said. "It creates a particular kind of suspense and a particular kind of tension."

9. The dialogue says it all.

Hartley pointed out that we tend to think of Shakespeare as a great philosopher, spouting off wisdoms—but that's not the case. "Every word in Shakespeare is dialogue. It comes from character. We do not know what Shakespeare thought about anything, and that's what makes him good."

10. Shakespeare was all about output.

"You want to learn from Shakespeare? Write a ton of stuff," Hartley said. On average, Shakespeare released the great works of literature at a rate of about two plays a year for two decades.

As a quick aside, *The Guardian* published a list of ten books based on Shakespeare's plays. This pretty much proves Rule Number 1.

1. Moby-Dick by Herman Melville (Macbeth/King Lear)
2. The Daughter of Time by Josephine Tey (Richard III)
3. Brave New World by Aldous Huxley (The Tempest)

4. Cakes and Ale by W Somerset Maugham (Twelfth Night)
5. The Talented Mr Ripley by Patricia Highsmith (Macbeth)
6. The Black Prince by Iris Murdoch (Hamlet)
7. The Dogs of War by Frederick Forsyth (Julius Caesar)
8. Wise Children by Angela Carter (The Taming of the Shrew et al)
9. Love in Idleness by Amanda Craig (A Midsummer Night's Dream)
10.   A Thousand Acres by Jane Smiley (King Lear)

◆ ◆ ◆

Chapter links

Ten Things Shakespeare Can Teach Us About Writing Thrillers

https://www.writersdigest.com/write-better-fiction/10-things-shakespeare-can-teach-us-about-writing-thrillers

Ten books based on Shakespeare's plays

https://www.theguardian.com/books/2014/

apr/30/top-10-novels-inspired-shakespeare-herman-melville-patricia-highsmith

3 — BENJAMIN FRANKLIN

Most Americans don't think of Benjamin Franklin as an author, yet for nearly thirty years, only the Bible outsold Poor Richard's Almanac, and his articles made the Pennsylvania Gazette the most successful newspaper in the colonies. Also, his autobiography has never been out of print. William Shakespeare, Charles Dickens, and Jane Austen have graced British notes, but Franklin is the only author to appear on American currency.

What advice did Franklin have for authors? In typical Franklin fashion, he imparted his advice by using an anecdote. On June 11, 1776, the second Continental Congress appointed a committee to write a declaration of independence. Thomas Jefferson, John Adams, Benjamin Franklin, Robert R. Livingston, and Roger Sherman were selected. At the time, Franklin was a renowned author but declined the offer to write the initial draft of the Declaration.

Jefferson reported that afterward, Franklin told him that he avoided drafting papers that would be reviewed by a public body. You can almost hear the seventy-year-old patriarch chuckling as he gave this advice to the young Virginian. According to Jefferson, Franklin told him the following story.

An apprentice hatter was about to open shop for himself. His first concern was to have a handsome signboard, with a proper inscription. He composed it in these words, "John Thompson, Hatter, makes and sells hats for ready money," with a figure of a hat subjoined. He then submitted it to friends for their amendments. The first he showed it to thought the word "Hatter" repetitive, because it was followed by the words "makes hats." It was struck out. The next observed that the word "makes" might as well be omitted, because his customers would not care who made the hats. He struck it out. A third said he thought the words "for ready money" were useless, as it was not the custom of the place to sell on credit. The inscription now stood, "John Thompson sells hats." "Sells hats!" says the next friend. "Why, nobody expects you to give them away. What then is the use of that word?" It was stricken out, and "hats" followed it, as there was one painted on the board. So the inscription was reduced to "John Thompson" with the figure of a hat subjoined.

That piece of writing advice is certainly worth a Benjamin.

4 — MARK TWAIN

Mark Twain didn't leave us a list of tips, but he wrote a review of James Fenimore Cooper's writing that contained eighteen ironclad writing rules. Twain was not a fan of Cooper's writing. Wait, that was far too mild of a sentence. In his article "Fenimore Cooper's Literary Offenses," Twain ridicules, lacerates, and skewers the poor man. Here's a sample.

> *Cooper's art has some defects. In one place in "Deerslayer," and in the restricted space of two-thirds of a page, Cooper has scored 114 offenses against literary art out of a possible 115. It breaks the record. There are nineteen rules governing literary art in domain of romantic fiction -- some say twenty-two. In "Deerslayer," Cooper violated eighteen of them.*

This 1895 article made me laugh out loud. Besides the humor, I saw something else in the article. If all his criticisms of Cooper were rewritten as positive statements, they would make a fine guide to great writing. (You can read the entire article by following the link at the end of this chapter.)

So, with clemency from Twain, I present Mark Twain's

18 Commandments of Writing

1. A tale shall accomplish something and arrive somewhere.

2. Episodes in a tale shall be necessary parts of the tale and shall help to develop it.

3. Personages in a tale shall be alive, except in the case of corpses, and that always the reader shall be able to tell the corpses from the others.

4. Personages in a tale, both dead and alive, shall exhibit a sufficient excuse for being there.

5. When the personages of a tale deal in conversation, the talk shall sound like human talk, and be talk such as human beings would be likely to talk in the given circumstances, and have a discoverable meaning, also a discoverable purpose, and a show of relevancy, and remain in the neighborhood of the subject at hand, and be interesting to the reader, and help out the tale, and stop when the people cannot think of anything more to say.

6. When the author describes the character of a personage in the tale, the conduct and conversation of that personage shall justify said descrip-

tion.

7. When a personage talks like an illustrated, gilt-edged, tree-calf, hand-tooled, seven- dollar Friendship's Offering in the beginning of a paragraph, he shall not talk like a Negro minstrel in the end of it.

8. Crass stupidities shall not be played upon the reader by either the author or the people in the tale.

9. Personages of a tale shall confine themselves to possibilities and let miracles alone; or, if they venture a miracle, the author must so plausibly set it forth as to make it look possible and reasonable.

10. The author shall make the reader feel a deep interest in the personages of his tale and in their fate; and that he shall make the reader love the good people in the tale and hate the bad ones.

11. Characters in a tale shall be so clearly defined that the reader can tell beforehand what each will do in a given emergency.

12. Say what he is proposing to say, not merely come near it.

13. Use the right word, not its second cousin.

14. Eschew surplusage.

15. Do not omit necessary details.

16. Avoid slovenliness of form.

17. Use good grammar.

18. Employ a simple and straightforward style.

Great list, huh? Anyway, I'll let Twain conclude with his final comments about Cooper.

I may be mistaken, but it does seem to me that "Deerslayer" is not a work of art in any sense; it does seem to me that it is destitute of every detail that goes to the making of a work of art; in truth, it seems to me that "Deerslayer" is just simply a literary delirium tremens. A work of art? It has no invention; it has no order, system, sequence, or result; it has no lifelike- ness, no thrill, no stir, no seeming of reality; its characters are confusedly drawn, and by their acts and words they prove that they are not the sort of people the author claims that they are; its humor is pathetic; its pathos is funny; its conversations are -- oh! Indescribable; its love- scenes odious; its English a crime against the ...nting these out, what is left is nust all admit that.

...to get on the bad side of Twain.

Curiosity.com published a somewhat different list of writing tips from Mark Twain. The source article is no longer available, but luckily, I preserved it for you. This list was culled from his letters.

1. Write without pay until somebody offers to pay.

2. Don't say the old lady screamed. Bring her on and let her scream.

3. Great books are weighed and measured by their style and matter, and not the trimmings and shadings of their grammar.

4. The time to begin writing an article is when you have finished it to your satisfaction.

5. If I had more time, it would have been shorter.

6. The more you explain it, the less I understand it.

7. Substitute 'damn' every time you're inclined to write 'very.' Your editor will delete it and the writing will be just as it should be.

8. The difference between the right word and the almost right word is the difference between lightning and a *lightning* bug.

9. Use plain, simple *language*, short words, a brief sentences... don't *let* fluff and flowers

verbosity creep in.

10.   As to the adjective: When in doubt, strike it out.

◆ ◆ ◆

Chapter Links

Fenimore Cooper's Literary Offenses by Mark Twain
http://twain.lib.virginia.edu/projects/rissetto/
offense.html

5 — GEORGE ORWELL

George Orwell only had six pieces of writing advice, but they are all gems. He might also have added that an honest writer should avoid Newspeak.

1. Never use a metaphor, simile, or other figure of speech which you are used to seeing in print.

2. Never use a long word where a short one will do.

3. If it is possible to cut a word out, always cut it out.

4. Never use the passive where you can use the active.

5. Never use a foreign phrase, scientific word, or jargon if you can think of an everyday English equivalent.

6. Break any of these rules sooner than say anything outright barbarous.

Orwell also had six questions he believed every author ought to ask themselves about their work.

These would pretty much take his advice count to an even dozen.

1. What am I trying to say?

2. What words will express it?

3. What image or idiom will make it clearer?

4. Is this image fresh enough to have an effect?

5. Could I put it more shortly?

6. Have I said anything that is avoidably ugly?

6 — STEPHEN KING

In a Barnes & Noble Book Blog, Stephen King presents 20 writing tips. Most famous writers offer ten or perhaps a dozen tips, but as you may have noticed, King is prolific. Stephen King is a great storyteller. His memoir, *On Writing: A Memoir of the Craft* contains a wealth of wisdom about writing and every serious writer ought to read it. This list is much shorter, but all writers can benefit from these guidelines.

1. First write for yourself, and then worry about the audience.

2. Don't use passive voice.

3. Avoid adverbs.

4. Avoid adverbs, especially after "he said" and "she said."

5. But don't obsess over perfect grammar.

6. The magic is in you.

7. Read, read, read.

8. Don't worry about making other people happy.

9. Turn off the TV.

10. You have three months.

11. There are two secrets to success.

12. Write one word at a time.

13. Eliminate distraction.

14. Stick to your own style.

15. Dig.

16. Take a break.

17. Leave out the boring parts and kill your darlings.

18. The research shouldn't overshadow the story.

19. You become a writer simply by reading and writing.

20. Writing is about getting happy.

Good advice. I especially like his comment in this interview that a writer's goal is "to make him/her forget, whenever possible, that he/she is reading a story at all."

Chapter Links

Stephen King interview at barnesandnoble.com.
https://www.barnesandnoble.com/blog/stephen-
kings-top-20-rules-for-writers/

7 — JOHN STEINBECK

Six tips on writing from Pulitzer Prize winner and Nobel laureate John Steinbeck.

1. Abandon the idea that you are ever going to finish. Lose track of the 400 pages and write just one page for each day, it helps. Then when it gets finished, you are always surprised.

2. Write freely and as rapidly as possible and throw the whole thing on paper. Never correct or rewrite until the whole thing is down. Rewrite in process is usually found to be an excuse for not going on. It also interferes with flow and rhythm which can only come from a kind of unconscious association with the material.

3. Forget your generalized audience. In the first place, the nameless, faceless audience will scare you to death and in the second place, unlike the theater, it doesn't exist. In writing, your audience is one single reader. I have found that sometimes it helps to pick out one person—a real person you know, or an imagined person and write to that one.

4. If a scene or a section gets the better of you and you still think you want it—bypass it and go on. When you have finished the whole you can come back to it and then you may find that the reason it gave trouble is because it didn't belong there.

5. Beware of a scene that becomes too dear to you, dearer than the rest. It will usually be found that it is out of drawing.

6. If you are using dialogue—say it aloud as you write it. Only then will it have the sound of speech.

8 — RAYMOND CHANDLER

Beyond great novels and screenplays, Chandler wrote about Hollywood and writing. It would be an understatement to say he disliked the tradition of English murder mysteries. Chandler liked realism, not puzzles.

Here are his 10 rules for mystery writing.

1. It must be credibly motivated, both as to the original situation and the dénouement.

2. It must be technically sound as to the methods of murder and detection.

3. It must be realistic in character, setting and atmosphere. It must be about real people in a real world.

4. It must have a sound story value apart from the mystery element: i.e., the investigation itself must be an adventure worth reading.

5. It must have enough essential simplicity to be explained easily when the time comes.

6. It must baffle a reasonably intelligent reader.

7. The solution must seem inevitable once revealed.

8. It must not try to do everything at once. If it is a puzzle story operating in a rather cool, reasonable atmosphere, it cannot also be a violent adventure or a passionate romance.

9. It must punish the criminal in one way or another, not necessarily by operation of the law.... If the detective fails to resolve the consequences of the crime, the story is an unresolved chord and leaves irritation behind it.

10.   It must be honest with the reader.

9 — ELMORE LEONARD

In 2009, The Western Writers of America presented Elmore Leonard with their prestigious Owen Wister Award for lifetime achievement. Leonard wrote *3:10 to Yuma, Hombre, Last Stand at Saber River*, and many other Westerns. He also wrote novels outside the Western genre, including *Get Shorty, Jackie Brown*, and *Out of Sight*.

Leonard published his *10 Rules of Writing* as a book, but it was not much more than a padded version of his *New York Times* article by the same name. The book can be panned for its brevity, but the advice is sound.

Leonard's ten rules for writing

1. Never open a book with weather.

2. Avoid prologues.

3. Never use a verb other than "said" to carry dialogue.

4. Never use an adverb to modify the verb "said."

5. Keep your exclamation points under control.

6. Never use the words "suddenly" or "all hell

broke out."

7. Use regional dialects, patois, sparingly.

8. Avoid detailed descriptions of characters.

9. Don't go into great detail describing places and things.

10.   Try to leave out the part that readers tend to skip.

◆ ◆ ◆

Chapter links

Elmore Leonard New York Times article
http://www.nytimes.com/2001/07/16/arts/
writers-writing-easy-adverbs-exclamation-points-
especially-hooptedoodle.html

10 — JENNIFER CODY EPSTEIN

Jennifer Cody Epstein published, "10 Rules for Rewriting History" at Writer Unboxed. The article is helpful and full of great advice. Epstein was specifically addressing historical fiction, but her tips are applicable to most genres.

1. History rides shotgun. Remember that what you're writing is a novel—not a history book. This means history should be used only to heighten and deepen your narrative, and not the other way around. If it doesn't relate to your plot, it shouldn't be in there.

2. Write right away. Many historical novelists put off writing until they feel that they've "researched enough." If your story is strong enough, though, you should be able to write it (or much of it) immediately.

3. Research like hell. The more you do the more authentic your book will feel. I probably read about twenty books for each novel, and countless online pages and papers.

4. The 30 Percent Rule: It's one of the depressing

realities of researching: the vast majority of it probably won't make your book. In my experience, I only use about 30% of what I've learned.

5. Talk to real people. I've found that some of my most vivid information comes from people, not pages—and that interviewing and observing subjects related to your story will add real-life nuance that text alone won't.

6. Watch out for big-shots. One of the coolest things about historical fiction is the writer's omnipotence: you can put anyone/thing anywhere you want them. Don't abuse it. On the other hand, including relevant smaller historical details will heighten your book's credibility.

7. Vet vernacular. One of the hardest tasks a historical writer faces is finding language that fits his time, place and characters. We are all the products of our respective eras and locales, and these things will inevitably creep into your narrative, so vet your language very carefully after you write it. Read it out loud to yourself, slowly.

8. Make a timeline. What major world and domestic events (like the Treaty of Versailles and China's May 4th Movement), and art trends (like the beginning of abstract painting) might have been in headlines and people's discussions.

9. Check your facts. It's incredibly important to get stuff right—with each mistake, you lose a lit-

tle more of your reader's faith. It's inevitable, of course, that some mistakes will slip through the net—historical fiction is particularly vulnerable in this area. If you're really in uncertain territory —as I often found myself in my novels—it's well worth it to hire an expert to read through.

10.   Free your mind. It may seem strange, but another hard part of fictionalizing history is just allowing yourself to fictionalize. If it can't be easily proven that something didn't happen, you can write as though it did.

◆ ◆ ◆

Chapter links

Jennifer Cody Epstein's 10 Rules for Rewriting History at *Writers Unboxed*

https:// writerunboxed.com/2014/01/19/10-rules-for-rewriting-history/

11 — KURT VONNEGUT

Here are Kurt Vonnegut's "8 Tips on How to Write a Great Story."

1. Use the time of a total stranger in such a way that he or she will not feel the time was wasted.

2. Give the reader at least one character he or she can root for.

3. Every character should want something, even if it is only a glass of water.

4. Every sentence must do one of two things — reveal character or advance the action.

5. Start as close to the end as possible.

6. Be a Sadist. No matter how sweet and innocent your leading characters, make awful things happen to them-in order that the reader may see what they are made of.

7. Write to please just one person. If you open a

window and make love to the world, so to speak, your story will get pneumonia.

8. Give your readers as much information as possible as soon as possible. To hell with suspense. Readers should have such complete understanding of what is going on, where and why, that they could finish the story themselves, should cockroaches eat the last few pages.

Chapter Links

Kurt Vonnegut four-minute definition of storytelling   http://www.youtube.com/watch?v=oP3c1h8v2ZQ)

12 — ERNEST HEMINGWAY

Hemingway never published advice for aspiring writers, but he spoke or wrote enough about writing that Larry W. Phillips was able to edit a collection of his reflections on the craft titled Ernest Hemingway on Writing.

Here are a dozen tips gleaned from Hemingway lifelong musings about writing.

1. Use short sentences.
2. Use short first paragraphs.
3. Use vigorous English.
4. Be positive, not negative.
5. To get started, write one true sentence.
6. Always stop for the day while you still know what will happen next.
7. Never think about the story when you're not working.
8. Don't describe an emotion–make it.
9. Be brief.
10. The first draft of everything is shit.
11. Prose is architecture, not interior decoration.
12. Write drunk, edit sober.

Chapter links

Larry W. Phillips' *Ernest Hemingway on Writing.* https://www.amazon.com/Ernest-Hemingway-Writing-Larry-Phillips-ebook/dp/B000FC0O1I/

13 — HENRY MILLER

As someone who admires storytelling, I'm not a fan of Henry Miller. He wrote stop-and-read-again sentences. Beautiful sentences. But stringing these sentences together with coherency seemed beyond his capabilities. I suspect he injected sex into his writing because deep in his heart, he knew he was boring. Miller reminds me of the comment by Steve Martin's character in *Planes, Trains, and Automobiles*, "And by the way, you know, when you're telling these little stories? Here's a good idea - have a point. It makes it so much more interesting for the listener!"

Despite my reservations, I'll include his writing advice because many believe that Henry Miller was a literary giant. In typical Miller fashion, he called these Commandments.

1. Work on one thing at a time until finished.

2. Don't be nervous. Work calmly, joyously, recklessly on whatever is in hand.

3. Work according to program and not according to mood. Stop at the appointed time!

4. When you can't create you can work.

5. Cement a little every day, rather than add new fertilizers.

6. Keep human! See people, go places, drink if you feel like it.

7. Don't be a draught-horse! Work with pleasure only.

8. Discard the program when you feel like it—but go back to it next day. Concentrate. Narrow down. Exclude.

9. Forget the books you want to write. Think only of the book you are writing.

10.   Write first and always. Painting, music, friends, cinema, all these come afterwards.

14 — ROAD RUNNER

Chuck Jones created 9 Golden rules for the *Road Runner* cartoons. These famous rules insured that fans received exactly what they expected from these Loony Tunes characters. First the rules, and then some storytelling lessons we can draw from this popular cartoon series.

Rule 1. The Road Runner cannot harm the coyote except by going "beep, beep!"

Rule 2. No outside force can harm the coyote —only his own ineptitude or the failure of the Acme products

Rule 3. The coyote can stop anytime—if he were not a fanatic. (Repeat: "A fanatic is one who redoubles his efforts when he has forgotten his aim." George Santayana)

Rule 4. No dialogue ever, except "Beep Beep!"

Rule 5. The Road Runner must stay on the road— otherwise logically he would not be called

Road Runner.

Rule 6. All action must be confined to the natural environment of the two characters—the Southwest American desert.

Rule 7. All material, tools, weapons, or mechanical conveniences must be obtained from the Acme Corporation.

Rule 8. Whenever possible, make gravity the coyote's greatest enemy.

Rule 9. The coyote is always more humiliated than harmed by his failures.

The first take-away from these rules is that you should do the same. If you write a series or a single novel, write down the plot and character rules. The protagonist must remain true to his or her character and the plot cannot go too far afield without losing fans. This little exercise brings clarity and dependability to stories.

The second take-away is eye-opening. Like the *Road Runner and Wile E. Cayote*, all stories revolve around an antagonist making life difficult for a protagonist. Many stories have multiple antagonists and/or protagonists. Then after these main characters, a story is usually populated with all sorts of supporting and bit players. All these characters communicate with each other through dialogue and gestures. But what if you were to whittle a story's essentials down to the absolute minimum? Could a story be told in a world populated by only one protagonist relentlessly pursued by a single antagonist? No other characters. Minimal dialogue. Steven Spielberg's first movie *Duel* shows this can be done, as does Tom Hanks' *Cast Away*. These are intimate, tense stories. *Road Runner* cartoons fits this minimalist construct. In fact, the *Road Runner* has no dialogue except for a single word repeated twice.

How in the world can you keep audience interest with these limitations? Watch a group of these Loony Tunes. You'll see pure essence of storytelling. Even if you have a cast of thousands, you can keep the reader's interest by following the precepts displayed so eloquently by The *Road Runner* cartoons.

15 — ROBERT A. HEINLEIN

Robert A. Heinlein was a science-fiction author, best known for *Stranger in a Strange Land*. He was referred to as the "dean of science fiction writers." Being a simple man, he only had five rules for writers.

1. You must write.
2. You must finish what you write.
3. You must refrain from rewriting, except to editorial order.
4. You must put the work on the market.
5. You must keep the work on the market until it is sold.

Perhaps facetious … perhaps not.

16 — AUTHOR QUOTES

"When a book, any sort of book, reaches a certain intensity of artistic performance it becomes literature. That intensity may be a matter of style, situation, character, emotional tone, or idea, or half a dozen other things. It may also be a perfection of control over the movement of a story similar to the control a great pitcher has over a ball." Raymond Chandler

"I think I did pretty well, considering I started out with nothing but a bunch of blank paper." Steve Martin

"A blank piece of paper is God's way of telling us how hard it to be God." Sidney Sheldon

"The best thing about writing fiction is that moment where the story catches fire and comes to life on the page, and suddenly it all makes sense and you know what it's about and why you're doing it and what these people are saying and doing, and you get to feel like both the creator and the audience. Everything is suddenly both obvious and surprising… and it's magic and wonderful and strange." Neil Gaiman

"Writing a book is an adventure. To begin with it is

a toy and amusement. Then it becomes a mistress, then it becomes a master, then it becomes a tyrant. The last phase is that just as you are about to be reconciled to your servitude, you kill the monster and fling him out to the public." Winston Churchill

"Give your readers as much information as possible as soon as possible. To hell with suspense. Readers should have such complete understanding of what is going on, where and why, that they could finish the story themselves, should cockroaches eat the last few pages." Kurt Vonnegut

"It took me fifteen years to discover I had no talent for writing, but I couldn't give it up because by that time I was too famous." Robert Benchley

"I have been successful probably because I have always realized that I knew nothing about writing and have merely tried to tell an interesting story entertainingly." Edgar Rice Burroughs

"First, find out what your hero wants, then just follow him!" Ray Bradbury

"Down these mean streets a man must go who is not himself mean, who is neither tarnished nor afraid. He is the hero; he is everything. He must be the best man in his world and a good enough man for any world. The story is this man's adventure in search of a hidden truth, and it would be no adventure if it did not happen to a man fit for adventure. If there were enough like him, the world would be a very safe place to live in, without becoming too dull to be worth living in." Raymond Chandler

"I love deadlines. I like the whooshing sound they make as they fly by." Douglas Adams

"Half my life is an act of revision." John Irving

"No iron can pierce the heart with such force as a period put just at the right place." Isaac Babel

"A tired exclamation mark is a question mark." Stanislaw Jerzy Lec

"Any word you have to hunt for in a thesaurus is the wrong word. There are no exceptions to this rule." Stephen King

"I'm all in favor of keeping dangerous weapons out of the hands of fools. Let's start with typewriters." Solomon Short

"Quantity produces quality. If you only write a few things, you are doomed." Ray Bradbury

"In a thousand words I can have the Lord's Prayer, the 23rd Psalm, the Hippocratic Oath, a sonnet by Shakespeare, the Preamble to the Constitution, Lincoln's Gettysburg Address and almost all of the Boy Scout Oath. Now exactly what picture were you planning to trade for all that?" Roy H. Williams

"Success comes to a writer, as a rule, so gradually that it is always something of a shock to him to look back and realize the heights to which he has climbed." P. G. Wodehouse

"A writer should have another lifetime to see if he's appreciated." Jorge Luis Borges

"Thou shalt not is soon forgotten, but Once upon a time lasts forever." Philip Pullman

"Good friends, good books and a sleepy conscience: this is the ideal life." Mark Twain

"Knowing you have something good to read before bed is among the most pleasurable of sensations." Vladimir Nabokov

"Reading is the sole means by which we slip, involuntarily, often helplessly, into another's skin, another's voice, another's soul." Joyce Carol Oates

"There is no friend as loyal as a book." Ernest Hemingway

"I am simply a 'book drunkard.' Books have the same irresistible temptation for me that liquor has for its devotee. I cannot withstand them." L.M. Montgomery

"It is what you read when you don't have to that determines what you will be when you can't help it." Oscar Wilde

"Be awesome! Be a book nut!" Dr. Seuss

"Good books, like good friends, are few and chosen; the more select, the more enjoyable." Louisa May

Alcott

"The one way of tolerating existence is to lose one-self in literature as in a perpetual orgy." Gustave Flaubert

"I cannot remember the books I've read any more than the meals I have eaten; even so, they have made me." Ralph Waldo Emerson

"I owe everything I am and everything I will ever be to books." Gary Paulsen

"Books are a uniquely portable magic." Stephen King

"Picking five favorite books is like picking the five body parts you'd most like not to lose." Neil Gaiman

"Reading brings us unknown friends." Honoré de Balzac

"When the Day of Judgment dawns and people, great and small, come marching in to receive their heavenly rewards, the Almighty will gaze upon the mere bookworms and say to Peter, "Look, these need no reward. We have nothing to give them. They have loved reading." Virginia Woolf

"Our favorite book is always the book that speaks most directly to us at a particular stage in our lives. And our lives change. We have other favorites that give us what we most need at that particular time. But we never lose the old favorites. They're always with us." Lloyd Alexander

"There are perhaps no days of our childhood we lived so fully as those we believe we left without having lived them, those we spent with a favorite book." Marcel Proust

"I have always imagined that Paradise will be a kind of library." Jorge Luis Borges

"It was books that taught me that the things that tormented me most were the very things that connected me with all the people who were alive, or who had ever been alive." James Baldwin

"It is so unsatisfactory to read a noble passage and have no one you love at hand to share the happiness with you." Mark Twain

"I cannot live without books." Thomas Jefferson

"Writing is the only thing that, when I do it, I don't feel I should be doing something else." Gloria Steinem

"You don't write because you want to say something; you write because you've got something to say." F. Scott Fitzgerald

Writing as a Contact Sport

Sometimes writers act badly toward other writers. Earlier we showed you that Mark Twain had some rather nasty thing to say about James Fenimore Cooper. Here are some additional zingers.

"Some editors are failed writers, but so are most writers." T. S. Eliot

"That's not writing, that's typing." Truman Capote to Jack Kerouac

"The world is rid of him, but the deadly slime of his touch remains." John Constable upon the death of Lord Byron

"Every word she writes is a lie, including 'and' and 'the.'" Mary McCarthy about Lillian Hellman

"If he really meant what he writes, he would not write at all." Gore Vidal about Henry Miller

"I am fairly unrepentant about her poetry. I really think that three quarters of it is gibberish. However, I must crush down these thoughts, otherwise the dove of peace will shit on me." Noel Coward about Dame Edith Sitwell

"He had a mind so fine that no idea could violate it." T. S. Eliot about Henry James

"She was a master at making nothing happen very slowly." Clifton Fadiman about Gertrude Stein

"The stupid person's idea of the clever person." Elizabeth Bowen about Aldous Huxley

"To those she did not like she was a stiletto made of sugar." John Mason Brown about Dorothy Parker

"To me Pound remains the exquisite showman without the show." Ben Hecht about Ezra Pound

"His verse is the beads without the string." Gerard Manley Hopkins about Robert Browning

"He is mad, bad and dangerous to know." Lady Caroline Lamb about Lord Byron

"Nothing but old fags and cabbage-stumps of quotations from the Bible and the rest, stewed in the juice of deliberate, journalistic dirty-mindedness." D. H. Lawrence about James Joyce

"He writes his plays for the ages - the ages between five and twelve." George Nathan about George Bernard Shaw

"Virginia Woolf's writing is no more than glamorous knitting. I believe she must have a pattern somewhere." Dame Edith Sitwell about Virginia Woolf

"A great zircon in the diadem of American literature." Gore Vidal about Truman Capote

"The only genius with an IQ of 60." Gore Vidal about Andy Warhol

"He is able to turn an unplotted, unworkable manuscript into an unplotted and unworkable manuscript with a lot of sex." Tom Volpe about Harold Robbins

17 — JAMES D. BEST

The previous tips dealt with writing fiction. My advice has more to do with revising fiction because great fiction is not written, it's rewritten. Unless you are a genius, revisions, edits, and polish are what will make your story soar.

Let's assume you have your first draft complete. Now what? Here are three goals for the second draft. You'll probably be flabbergasted I call them the three Cs.

1. Continuity

2. Clarity

3. Crispness

Continuity

In film, a script supervisor makes sure the placement of furniture is consistent from scene to scene. Novels need similar scrutiny. During this revision, I keep an eye out for characters getting up from a chair more than once or magically changing rooms, clothing, or weapons. I also review each character's dialogue to make sure what they say is consistent with their character. Last, I review the timeline to make sure I haven't excessively compressed or expanded time.

Clarity

Oftentimes an author knows exactly what he intended, but a reader goes, "huh?" Making things crystal clear alternately means adding a bit of explanation or deleting extraneous description that might lead the reader down a false path. Clarity also means making sure the reader knows who is talking. This can be especially confusing when there are more than two people in a conversation.

Crispness

Good narratives move crisply. Sometimes this means deleting a sentence that interferes with a smooth flow, but it usually means deleting superfluous words. I think of this process as removing speed bumps and filling in potholes. Ideally, every word, sentence and paragraph should move the story forward.

The Fun Part

A friend of mine unintentionally changed my attitude toward revisions. He restores antique cars and starts each project with barely more than a chassis and some rusted sheet metal. With utmost care, he painstakingly replaces every single part until his re-creation is better than the shiny piece of the American dream that was driven off the showroom. When he finishes, we go on a ride and I can tell he enjoys the envious looks and honks from other car enthusiasts.

After these inaugural rides, I always assumed the cars were finished, but every time I visited, he would be in the garage replacing this piece or that piece. If he weren't installing a newly acquired part, he would be polishing nooks and crannies that no one in a standing position would ever see. Sometimes I'd come over to find that he had painted the car a different color or replaced perfectly good upholstery.

One day I asked him if he ever tired of constantly changing an already beautiful car.

"Hell no," he said. "Building the car is work. This is the fun part."

"The fun part?"

"Whenever I start a new project car, I look forward to the day when the basic restoration is done so I can perfect it. My joy is in making it flawless. I fix the little details, so people love to spend time with my creation."

"But you keep working on it. How do you know when it's perfect?"

"One day I'll walk all around it, open the doors, lift the hood, examine the truck and there won't be any more changes I want to make." He shrugged. "Then I sell it and start all over again."

Now I look forward to completing a first draft manuscript so I can tighten and polish it until there are no more changes I want to make.

Then I sell it and start all over again.

CONCLUSION

There's a problem with these lists. If hard rules were all that was necessary to become a great writer, then we'd be awash in breathtaking literature. We have writing tips, rules, and guidelines aplenty, yet they don't seem to convey the masters' magic. What gives? All the rules are good advice, but first there must be compelling content.

I used to golf until I realized I only pretended to enjoy the game. Prior to making this discovery, with two friends I took a lesson from a teaching pro. We spent a couple hours on the range and putting green. Lots and lots of tips and advice. My head was swimming. I couldn't get my grip right for fear my backswing was too fast.

The all-day lesson included a round of golf with the teaching pro. We presumed he would critique our play as we went along. No way. On the first tee, he told us he wouldn't comment on our play until we were ensconced in the clubhouse for refreshments. He said we should forget everything he had told us. Forget it all. His advice was meant for the driving range and putting green. He reiterated that as we played this round, we were not to worry about grip, swing, or stance. We should concentrate on one thing and one thing only—keep our eye on the ball. Simple. Keep focused on the primary basic of all the basics. It was a fun round of golf with one of my lowest scores.

My point is that when you write a first draft, forget the rules. Focus solely on the story. Telling a great story is the real magic the masters mastered. Don't pull out the rules until you start the second draft, then apply them ruthlessly on the third and fourth draft. Hone and polish your manuscript until it's as bright as your future.

APPENDIX

THE WRITER'S TOOLBOX

Every craft requires tools. Luckily, writers only need two.

Merriam-Webster's Collegiate Dictionary
Your book is in here. Some assembly required.

The Chicago Manual of Style
Your assembly instructions.

THANK YOU

Also by James D. Best

The Shopkeeper
Leadville
Murder at Thumb Butte
The Return
Jenny's Revenge
Crossing the Animas
No Peace
The Shut Mouth Society
Deluge
The Templar Reprisals
Tempest at Dawn
Principled Action, Lessons from the Origins
of the American Republic
The Digital Organization

See further thoughts on writing at: jamesdbest.b-logspot.com

Visit and download book samples at my Author Page at Amazon

To be notified when I have a new book, please join my mailing list by sending me a note at jimbest@jamesdbest.com.

You can also receive email updates from my blog at http://jamesdbest.blogspot.com by leaving your email address in the Follow by Email box. Thanks again

www.ingramcontent.com/pod-product-compliance
Lightning Source LLC
Chambersburg PA
CBHW061728250726
48657CB00002B/835